Trio

Three Lambs, the Seasons of
Life and a Juniper Tree

RITA CECILIA HUIE

WestBow Press books may be ordered through booksellers or by contacting:

WestBow Press
A Division of Thomas Nelson & Zondervan
1663 Liberty Drive
Bloomington, IN 47403
www.westbowpress.com
844.714.3454

Because of the dynamic nature of the Internet, any web addresses or links contained in this book may have changed since publication and may no longer be valid. The views expressed in this work are solely those of the author and do not necessarily reflect the views of the publisher, and the publisher hereby disclaims any responsibility for them.

Any people depicted in stock imagery provided by Getty Images are models, and such images are being used for illustrative purposes only.
Certain stock imagery © Getty Images.

Interior Image Credit: Rita Cecilia Huie

Scripture marked (KJV) taken from the King James Version of the Bible.

Scripture quotations marked (NIrV) are taken from the Holy Bible, New International Reader's Version®, NIrV® Copyright © 1995, 1996, 1998, 2014 by Biblica, Inc.™ Used by permission of Zondervan. All rights reserved worldwide. www.zondervan.comThe "NIrV" and "New International Reader's Version" are trademarks registered in the United States Patent and Trademark Office by Biblica, Inc.™

ISBN: 978-1-6642-0613-7 (sc)
ISBN: 978-1-6642-0614-4 (e)

Library of Congress Control Number: 2020918184

Print information available on the last page.

WestBow Press rev. date: 03/16/2021

WESTBOW
PRESS®
A DIVISION OF THOMAS NELSON
& ZONDERVAN

DEDICATION:

For Mère who loved sheep watching till the end of her days

It was in the middle of Summer when Mom & Pop bought a farm in north central Texas. There were three lambs who were born on the land and tamed to like people. Their names were Boaz, Leah, and Sarah. Boaz and Sarah were fluffy white Dorper sheep, and Leah had spots of tan, brown, reddish brown, and gold like a *Coat of Many Colors*. (from Genesis 37:3, KJV) Leah had less wool than Boaz and Sarah, but not enough to knit a scarf.

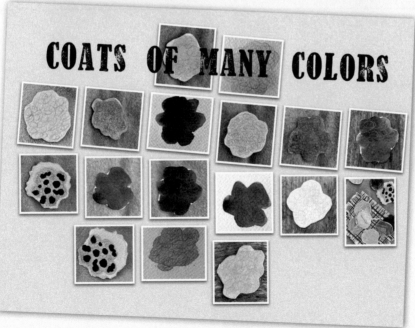

COATS OF MANY COLORS

When the Farm gets very hot, pink, orange and white wild flowers of spring dry up and purple thistles pop up all over the land. The sky gets true blue with a few white clouds, and there are pink and lavender hues in the early morning or late evening. The sun makes the ground very dry and the sheep have to work hard at finding grass to eat. They eat for 8 hours, play and rest for 8 hours, and sleep for 8 hours under a big juniper tree whose leaves and branches remain forest green like a Christmas Tree all year long. Before they go to sleep, all of the sheep walk in line to a big container of fresh water.

When fall comes, the brown, gold, red and dark green leaves start to fall and pumpkins line the many farm houses. Cool breezes start to blow through red-gold trees over colorful tawny hills. Fall is when Sarah and Leah had their first baby lambs. The new lambs brought joy and happiness to Mom & Pop. They called everyone they knew to announce the births of these fluffy babies and named them as if they were their children.

Leah's first baby lamb was called "Beignet". In the city of New Orleans where Mom came from before moving to the farm in Texas, she used to love to eat "beignet's" (pronounced "ben yays".) These are small, square fluffy donuts loaded with dollops of powdered sugar. Beignet looked like she was covered with powdered sugar so Pop decided to name her after the famous donut. Meanwhile Sarah had twins and their names were Sugar and Spice.

BEIGNETS

Then winter came and it grew colder and colder as the mothers kept their babies warm under wooly coats. They ate leaves from the fallen tree branches and watched rabbits, fox and deer run across the golden field that turned white during a snowfall. The sheep's water container froze and Pop had to break up the ice with a big stick so the thirsty sheep could drink. Mom played the Seasons of Antonio Vivaldi on her flute in the window by the fireside while watching the sheep in the snow.

WINTER MUSIC

In the spring, bluebonnets and lilies and plum blossoms were the first flowers to pop up. Mom and Pop took a long drive south to buy two new baby lambs. Chicory and Chanel were solid black, but later Chicory would grow a brown furry coat with very big horns.

More babies were born and things got very confusing. There were more triplets . One was gold, one was gray and one was white. There were more twins. Sonia and Gloria were named after Mom's twin aunts who died many years ago. There were some with tiny dots called nonpareils like the candy.

Leah and Sarah continued to have so many babies that Mom and Pop lost count! Chanel wanted to be a mother too and gave birth to black lambs with white dots. The farm eventually grew into a field of multi-colorful lambs. Some were white with black faces. Some had big spots like a cow, and others had stars and stripes. Some had fluffy coats and others had smooth coats.

A few years later, Leah grew older and tired. She closed her eyes and three lamb angels carried her up to Lamb Heaven as she turned whiter than snow. Her multicolored coat faded into a soft yellow white into the sky. One year later Boaz also grew very tired. Pop was surprised because Boaz was big and strong. He didn't feel very well as he lay down in a big hay bale and closed his eyes. Pop was very sad because Boaz was like a son.

Meanwhile Chanel and Sarah continued to have more and more baby lambs, and their daughter lambs were having them too, so it got to be even more confusing. Sarah, the matriarch of the sheep family, was a very good mother and grandmother for many lambs. But she finally grew older and slowed down. One winter leading into spring, she continued to walk around for many weeks trying to eat and drink. Mom and Pop were sad because they didn't think she would live much longer. When she got very sick they gave her some medicine and she drank a little water and laid down. The next morning there was a surprise! Sarah walked around for three more days eating and drinking and singing "baaaa's" for Mom and Pop! But the day finally came to join Boaz and Leah so she closed her eyes in the middle of the field under the juniper tree in the tall grasses. Three angel lambs came to deliver her up through the clouds. The Trio would be together again somewhere high above the farm.

The seasons of life continue on and on and the juniper tree gets taller and full of green leaves to provide plenty of shade in the summer. The flowers bloom in late spring and summer. Rain and snow cover the field. Sarah looks out for her sheep with Boaz and Leah. The Trio are complete in Lamb Heaven with their many ancestors looking over the large and continually growing flock of the field with love from above clouds in the golden pink and lavender sky.

I am the good shepherd. I know my sheep and my sheep know me, said the Lord . John 10:14. (NIRV)

VOCABULARY

Ancestors. Parents, grandparents, great grandparents, and further on.

Antonio Vivaldi. An Italian composer and Catholic priest in the early 1700s.

Beignet. A fried donut served with powdered sugar in New Orleans.

Boaz, Leah & Sarah. Names are from three Bible family stories.

Coat of Many Colors. A story in the Bible about Joseph's coat to represent God's light from Genesis 37:3, KJV

Descendants. Offspring, or children of.

Dollop. Scoop of whipped cream or big serving of a topping.

Dorper. A type of lamb with fluffy white wool.

Hues. Color shades.

Juniper. A cedar tree that grows naturally in Texas. In the Bible, the juniper tree is called a Broom Tree with a passage in Kings.

Lambs. Baby Sheep. Many references to Lambs in the Bible are about Jesus, the Lamb of God, and Sheep as His followers.

Matriarch. Older mother or grandmother of a family.

Nonpareil. Chocolate candy with white sugar dots.

Tawny. Fall colors: Beige, brown, gold, red, tan, yellow.

Trio. A set of three. In music, three instruments playing or three voices singing.

Music printed from: **The Four Seasons Complete,** (Antonio Vivaldi, 1678- 1741) for flute and piano, edited by James Galway (2011). *We carefully walk on the ice. We are afraid we may fall. We get up bravely and try again,* from Concerto in F minor, *Winter.*

Printed in the United States
by Baker & Taylor Publisher Services